THE
PEOPLE'S
MANIFESTO

MARK THOMAS

PRESENTS

THE

PEOPLE'S
MANIFESTO

EBURY
PRESS

5 7 9 10 8 6 4

Published in 2010 by Ebury Press, an imprint of Ebury Publishing
A Random House Group Company

The Random House Group Limited Reg. No. 954009

Addresses for companies within the Random House Group can be found at
www.randomhouse.co.uk

A CIP catalogue record for this book is available from the British Library

The Random House Group Limited supports The Forest Stewardship
Council (FSC), the leading international forest certification organisation.
All our titles that are printed on Greenpeace approved FSC certified paper
carry the FSC logo. Our paper procurement policy can be found at
www.rbooks.co.uk/environment

Designed and set by seagulls.net

Printed in the UK by CPI Cox & Wyman, Reading, RG1 8EX

ISBN 9780091937966

To buy books by your favourite authors and register for offers visit
www.rbooks.co.uk

INTRODUCTION

This Manifesto started as a live show, and the idea for the
show was simple. At the beginning of 2009 we were in
the middle of an economic crisis. Banks and countries
collapsed catastrophically, costing us £1.3 trillion, which
we paid to the very people who caused the problem in the
first place, while an illiberal and reactionary Labour
government twitched in its death throes and an illiberal
and reactionary Tory Party waited for their moment. The
words 'creek', 'without' and 'paddle' seemed to keep crop-
ping up. So the plan was this: I would ask my audiences
round the country for their ideas and policies to get us out
of the creek, in the sure knowledge that most people think

they could run the country better than any government and would be happy to share their opinions.

Each audience was given forms and asked for their policy ideas, grand or small, to change the world. The campaigning group NO2ID kindly organised volunteers to collect the suggestions and deliver them to me backstage, where each night I would read every one, weed out the doubles, put those that needed professional help to one side, and try to make sense of the rest.

Then, clutching 60 to 80 bits of paper, I launched myself onstage to discuss the policies, and each night the audience voted for their favourite idea; this was conducted using the advanced scientific method of 'who shouts loudest'. It's not the most rigorous method but I never needed to call on UN monitors, as the audience left me in no doubt if they thought I had not reflected their wishes.

Ideas were often specific to the area – Hull, for example, wanted to abolish the Humber toll bridge. In Norfolk they wanted more 'feral chicken roundabouts to calm traffic'. (There is already a feral chicken roundabout on the A142 at the Bungay and Ditchingham bypass where wild birds have lived and bred for over 50 years. Locals believe that drivers slow down at the roundabout so they don't hit the chickens crossing the road. This, I was assured, was Normal for Norfolk.)

Not every idea was grand. Some policies definitely focused on the small vexations of life:

> *Everyone has the right to use a product without having to reference a user manual.*

> *Mayonnaise should not be used as a moisturiser for sandwiches. It has no nutritional value and is the work of the devil, whose real name is Hell Man. Ban TV programmes about cooking, houses and meerkats.*

The word 'fuck' should be included in the automatic text/dictionary on mobile phones.

Ban golf umbrellas in cities.

Some of the policies fixated on celebrities, and although I am sure Jeremy Clarkson doesn't care what my audiences think of him, he should worry just a little bit in case any of them actually try and enact their suggestions. Each night produced a handful of what became known as 'celebrity death suggestions' but my favourite concerned Noel Edmonds. It simply read:

Noel Edmonds should be publicly beheaded and his severed head placed in one of 22 sealed red boxes.

Unsurprisingly many policies reflected public anger at bankers and MPs, but 4x4 drivers featured a lot too:

4x4 drivers should be forced to drive everywhere off-road, even to Sainsbury's.

4x4 drivers should be forced to drive their vehicle sitting on the roof in a deckchair with a long steering column.

Anyone with a 4x4 in a city must also volunteer for the nearest mountain rescue service.

As did the Olympics:

To save money and the environment, instead of the Olympics being held in one country, people could run around in circles in their own country at the same time.

The Olympics are too costly and will really cripple

our economy for little return. Why not give them
to the French?

As we are paying for them, any British citizen should
be eligible to enter any of the Olympic events.

Every night there would be ideas that genuinely took me,
and most of the audience, by surprise. One chap in Leicester wrote:

Everything in supermarkets should be stacked in
alphabetical order.

Pondering a world where Hovis would be found next to
Hobnobs or coffee next to cotton wool, I congratulated
this chap, saying that I thought his policy was very funny.
He fixed me firmly with a glare and said, 'It's not funny,
it's serious. I can't find anything.'

Not all the policies voted through were ones I agreed with, and some nights I found myself at odds with the proposers and indeed the audience. In Darlington the policy that won that evening was: 'Institute the Sky test on benefit claimants, so if you suck on the teat of Murdoch, no benefits for you.' Basically, if you are unemployed and have Sky, you get your benefits cut. I said to the chap who proposed it, 'You can't tell people on the dole what to do with their dole money.' 'I work in the benefits office,' he replied, 'and I can tell you now that a basic Murdoch Sky package is about £4 a week. Jobseeker's Allowance is £64.30. So if you are unemployed and have Sky, that is a subsidy of the Murdoch empire from the taxpayer via the unemployed at a rate of over 6 per cent of their benefit a week.' Staggered by his precision, I replied, 'Well, I still don't think you should tell people how to spend their dole money.' 'But,' he said with a grin, 'if you campaign on this and are even halfway successful, you will force the *Sun* to

run a counter-campaign arguing for the right of the unemployed to sit on their arses and watch telly. And I have to
admit, that nearly won me over.

The audience was the ultimate jury for the ideas and
shows often became rowdy affairs; good points would see
the crowd cheer and clap, while other times audience
members argued with each other and once or twice I had
to break it up. The rules were created as we went along,
but audiences roughly voted for ideas on wit, ingenuity
and appropriateness (though not in that order). In
London one chap suggested:

*We should abolish all criminal laws in this country
and replace them with two offences.*

1) Being out of order

2) Being bang out of order

This received the best reaction to a policy all night – the audience clapped loudly and indeed he had to take a bow – but his policy did not win the vote. Neither did the man in Hemel Hempstead who got a great reaction to:

> *All cash point machines should have a GAMBLE*
> *button, so if we can't get enough out we still have*
> *a chance of affording what we want.*

What I loved was that audiences could be discussing something quite serious one minute and talking about yoghurt flavours the next. We could be exploring the idea that car parking fines should be based upon a car's value and then be arguing about what colour salt and vinegar crisp packets should be.[1] We'd be debating the merits of a policy that read:

Employers have to afford maternity and paternity leave; they should also give time off for conception leave,

and move on to:

Extend the sex discrimination act to the church and all religions.

Many performers say that they couldn't have done it without the audience, but I really couldn't. So thank you to everyone who came along to the show. I especially want to thank the audience in Canterbury. When they heard I would attempt to campaign on policies that got voted through, they kindly opted for:

MPs' expenses should be printed in the local paper every two weeks and constituents get to vote on whether they are accepted or not.

Which thankfully narrowly won over the close rival:

We should disguise leopards as foxes to fuck up the gentry.

This is the People's Manifesto as chosen by audiences around Britain. Each policy in this booklet was created, selected and shouted for at these shows. Whether it will end up in the British Library next to the Communist Party Manifesto or the *Rights of Man* remains to be seen.

Mark Thomas, December 2009

1

PARTY MANIFESTOS SHOULD BE LEGALLY BINDING

HOW DO WE make MPs do what we want them to do, short of donating money to the party coffers or through the more traditional method of sleeping with them? One solution is to make political manifestos legally binding.

When MPs fail to honour their election pledges, there are a limited number of things we can do about it. We can name and shame them in the press (though for that to really work requires your MP to attend a series of shame-awareness workshops); we can lobby them, protest and even beg them. But nothing really motivates an MP quite like the sight of a smiling lawyer.

I asked a smiling lawyer what she thought of this policy. She replied, 'I have one word to say on the prospect of taking MPs to court: "Kerching!"'

Unsurprisingly there is little support from MPs for this policy. Despite spending much of their time devising new ways of getting us into court, they don't relish the prospect of ending up there themselves. They give two arguments against. Firstly, that the ultimate sanction against an MP is the ballot box at the next election – meaning once elected, an MP is unaccountable to the public for the next five years, not to mention that in safe seats there is little chance of removing an incumbent MP short of catching them dressed as Osama bin Laden while buggering sheep in a telephone box, and in certain rural areas even then it's not guaranteed.

Their second argument is that in politics 'stuff happens', the unexpected occurs, forcing governments to reprioritise. To an extent this is true and to a greater extent, it is an utter cop-out. The answer is a fixed number of key pledges that are legally binding, each pledge costed, planned and timetabled, with the prospect of legal action being like a penalty clause on a building project.

A good practice run could be the mayoral manifesto of Boris Johnson. He pledged to 'act immediately to provide long-term funding for four Rape Crisis centres in London'. He would do this by 'cutting the number of GLA spin doctors' to find the '£744,000 which would fund our commitment to dramatically increasing access to support services for rape victims'.[2] This funding was to be annual. Johnson took over City Hall on 4 May 2008. After being publicly embarrassed, Johnson finally got £265,000 to one centre in November 2009, but at the time of writing the rest of the money still hasn't appeared.

It took a year and a half and a lot of public pressure to get less than a quarter of the money promised in the manifesto: wouldn't a little court order nudge things along?

Either fully fund the centres or Boris Johnson ends up in cuffs in the back of a van. Like most I would prefer the former but the latter has its upside.

2

SHUT DOWN
TAX HAVENS ...
BOMB SWITZERLAND

IT IS IMPORTANT to bomb Switzerland if only to prove that just because you're neutral it doesn't mean anyone likes you. In any case, the Swiss were bankers to Nazi gold and hoarded art works, which in my book doesn't count as 'staying out of it'. Not so much being neutral as being service providers for fascism.

The real issue here is tax. Switzerland is one of the biggest tax havens in the world, so financially advantageous that bombing it is probably tax-deductible. You might even be eligible for a rebate. The low tax rates (and in some cases no tax rates) for businesses, added to legendary banking secrecy laws to hide behind, make tax havens the financial pirate coves for multinationals, tax dodgers and corrupt politicians. Her Majesty's Revenue and Customs loses about £18.5 billion each year to offshore tax evasion, tax avoidance and corporate tax 'efficiencies'.[3]

Benefit cheats cost the UK taxpayer £900 million in 2009,[4] a fraction of the money lost through offshore tax havens – money that could be spent on hospitals, schools and duck houses.

Switzerland is only the start. There are 60 tax havens (or 'secrecy jurisdictions' as they are becoming increasingly known) around the world, and Britain has jurisdiction over or strong influence on a staggering 31 of them.

Three are British dependencies: Guernsey, Jersey, the Isle of Man.

Seven are British Overseas Territories: Anguilla, Bermuda, British Virgin Islands, Cayman Islands, Gibraltar, Montserrat, Turks and Caicos Islands.

Twenty-one are members of the Commonwealth of Nations (formerly the British Commonwealth): Antigua and Barbuda, Bahamas, Barbados, Belize, Brunei, Cook Islands, Cyprus, Dominica, Grenada, Labuan, Maldives,

Malta, Mauritius, Nauru, Seychelles, Singapore, St Kitts and Nevis, St Lucia, St Vincent and the Grenadines, City of London (UK),Vanuatu.

Britain could start to shut them down through diplomacy, but when did it become British policy to solve problems diplomatically when there is a chance of a fight? Bomb Switzerland and the rest will shut down automatically. What has Switzerland got that is so indispensable to the world? Fondue, luxury pralines and yodelling, that is what. If you like chocolate, cheese and shouting in gangs, you can find it at any bus stop in Croydon at 3.30 on a school day.

'Ah,' you may cry, 'every country has a tourist selling point.' Indeed, and Switzerland's is assisted suicide.

3

MODELS SHOULD BE CHOSEN AT RANDOM FROM THE ELECTORAL ROLL

GET A MENTAL image of your grandfather sitting down for breakfast. The radio is on and steam gently rises from a cup of tea. In front of him is a half-eaten boiled egg and some buttered bread. He opens the morning post and as he reads his eyebrows raise until he splutters, 'Bloody hell, I've got to go and model Calvin Klein pants tomorrow!' Now imagine him standing bare-chested in baggy-fit jeans with his pants pulled right up to show the brand logo on the elasticated band. Finally imagine walking past the billboard advert of your grandad in those pants. This, then, is the full glory of this policy: the selection of models is left to chance and we end up with anyone and everyone sashaying down the catwalk in Milan and Paris.

Instead of an idealised vision of what is erotic or beautiful, airbrushed and primped by the fashion industry and supported by a modelling industry predicated upon eating disorders, we get to see our lives and bodies reflected back at us. And at that point we rewrite the rule book for what society deems to be beautiful.

This policy was chosen in London, but it harks back to another policy suggestion from an audience member in Hull. Roundly cheered when it was read out, it simply declared that 'we should take fashion designers outside and bash them into the shape they think we're in'. Although both policies have certain merits, the random selection of models causes designers far greater pain than mere physical violence – imagine the mental anguish of having to create haute couture at size 22.

This policy would also apply to magazine and TV adverts, and would include any celebrity modelling too. So a Porsche advert might feature a mum from a semi in Wokingham. Expensive watches normally seen next to aviator-style sunglasses and polo mallets end up hanging on the wrist of your local postman. Even the Argos catalogue would have to actually choose models at random, instead of merely trying to give the impression it had.

M&S knickers would not be advertised by Twiggy and some young thin things; it could be a student who has just come back from a gap year in Thailand, your mum, and a 25-year-old woman with Down's Syndrome. The size zero debate ends here. And beauty becomes something that we no longer aspire to but that we just have.

The slightly tricky question about this policy is, should it apply to porn? The answer has to be yes. It might also be an idea to make the selection process non-gender specific, and certainly non-age-specific. I think my older self would enjoy the prospect of getting a letter from *Razzle* informing me of my selection for their latest shoot, as I pottered around an old people's home in slippers and a T-shirt bearing the words 'WILL FUCK FOR BISCUITS'.

4

IT SHOULD BE LEGAL FOR GAY COUPLES TO GET MARRIED

IN A FAIR society it is only right and proper that gay couples have the mundanity of marriage inflicted upon them the same as everyone else. What makes them so special that they get let off? It is patently absurd that just because you and your partner share the same type of genitals you should escape the living hell of organising flowers, invites, seating, eating, dresses, cars, in-laws, out-laws and crap discos.

In that same spirit we should go one step further and allow heterosexual couples to have civil partnerships, for those people who still enjoy great sex but don't want to get a joint mortgage. This would enable heterosexual couples to boldly declare to the world: 'I love you, I'm moving in with you but I'm still keeping the flat on.'

Many who object to gay marriage say homosexuality is not 'natural'. Neither is hair dye, UHT milk or the closet freezer. If you want to return to an era where nature ruled then we would only use plant medicine, our life expectancy would be about 40 and anyone living longer would be seen as a degenerate. Bigots would moan, 'I've got nothing against pensioners personally, I just don't want my father turning into one.'

Those who object to gay marriage on religious grounds often cite the book of Leviticus in the Bible, which says, 'If a man lies with a man as with a woman, both of them have committed an abomination' (Lev 20:13).

However, in Leviticus God also decrees that menstruating women should be kept separate for seven days and on the eighth day that woman should sacrifice two pigeons to make herself clean again (Lev 15:29), that these pigeons should have their necks wrung by a priest at the altar, the feathers cast to the east side of the altar and the pigeon then burnt on the altar itself (Lev 1:13–16). Despite these clear instructions from the Bible, there have been no recorded sightings of religious groups offering free fowl with every pack of Tampax.

(Or perhaps in certain religious circles women, finding themselves caught out, sidle up to other women and whisper, 'Er, has anyone got a spare pigeon in their handbag? I've just come off.')

So, the Bible has been used selectively to back an argument against gay couples. Unusual, that.

5

**PEOPLE WHO ALLOW
THEIR DOG TO SHIT
ON THE PAVEMENT
WITHOUT CLEANING IT
UP SHOULD BE FORCED
TO WEAR IT AS A
MOUSTACHE**

WE ARE A nation on the brink of apoplexy induced by dog crap. Nothing, it seems, can bring on a brain-bursting fit of fury faster than the sight of a nonchalant dog owner failing to clear up their canine's cable. Every single night the audience had suggestions of what punishment should be meted out to hapless hound owners. Here is just a small sample of them:

'If a dog owner lets their dog shit on your doorstep you should be able to shit on theirs.'

'Change the law so if someone allows their dog to shit on your doorstep, then you should be able to shit upon their head.' I challenged the policy proposer, saying this law would require the police to hold the offender down while the householder, publicly and to order, produced a revenge stool upon his or her head. The proposer was adamant that that would not be a problem.

'Dog owners who don't pick up their dog shit should be put in public stocks and have dog shit thrown at them' was another suggestion. Someone even proposed that 'we should include a luminous dye in dog food' so that we could spot piles glowing in the dark and thus avoid them. On hearing this, another audience member suggested an amendment. It read: 'Like the idea for the luminous dog food but shouldn't we include some kind of microchip bleeper to warn blind people.' On two separate occasions people have actually suggested that we set up a dog DNA register, a multi-million-pound dog-turd database, so police could work backwards to track down the offender, starting at the scene of the crime, complete with cordoned-off area, a little white tent and forensic experts in hooded bodysuits.

In Hastings the policy adopted was that 'people who allow their dog to shit on the pavement without cleaning it up should be forced to wear it as a moustache'. So upon catching sight of the offender, police should move in, saying, 'Is that your turd, sir? That's it, on the top lip, sir ... for the rest of the day.'

And the rest of us could point at them and say, 'Oh, look, a white moustache, you don't see that as often as you used to.'

6

MPS SHOULD NOT BE PAID
WAGES BUT LOANS, LIKE
STUDENTS, BECAUSE THEY
GET HIGHLY PAID JOBS
AFTER THEY GRADUATE
FROM WESTMINSTER AS
A RESULT OF ATTENDING
PARLIAMENT. THEY
SHOULD THEREFORE
PAY BACK THE LOAN
THEY RECEIVED WHILE
IN OFFICE

IN THE PANTHEON of heroes of British democracy, amidst the Suffragettes and the Putney Debates, stand the Chartists, a working-class movement in the nineteenth century founded upon six demands:

1. The vote
2. The ballot
3. Abolishing the need for a man to own property in order to stand as an MP
4. Equal-sized constituencies
5. Annual Parliaments

The Chartists agitated, petitioned, marched, demonstrated, were imprisoned, rebelled, rioted, fought and died for these rights, and for their sixth demand too:

6. Payment for MPs

Without a salary, the Chartists argued, only the rich could afford to be MPs and thus the toffs got to stay in power regardless of who had the vote. Paying MPs a salary was regarded as fundamental to democracy. So the Chartists would approve of our current MPs getting a salary – but I am willing to bet that no Chartist ever thought, I may be facing death by hanging but one day, thanks to my sacrifice, MPs will be able to claim duck houses on expenses.

As the policy says, MPs often get highly paid jobs as a result of attending Parliament, so consider Patricia Hewitt MP (Lab – Leicester).

According to the Register of Members' Interests, Patricia's total earnings were £198,000 in 2009/10. She augments her MP's salary of £64,766 with a series of other jobs, including working as a special consultant for Boots the Chemist (Alliance Boots Ltd) for which she is paid £45,000 a year. Now, seriously, does anyone think she would have got the job with Boots had she not been health minister?

Patricia is also a senior adviser for Cinven Ltd (the offshore venture capitalists who bought private health company BUPA), for which she is paid £55,000 a year.[5] Now, perhaps it is too cynical to believe that she got that job because of her ministerial past with the Department of Health. Perhaps she didn't even mention it and just did a really good interview.

This policy may not be the panacea or a silver bullet for the problems with Parliamentary democracy but it would serve as a reminder that MPs work for our betterment not theirs. Not to mention the fact that the prospect of MPs having to pay money back to the public purse will put the fear of fucking God into them, and that in itself is all the validation this policy needs.

7

LEGALISE ALL DRUGS

IN ESSENCE, PROHIBITION is not a policy but a wish. Declaring drugs illegal will not make them go away any more than making unicorns legal will make them appear. Prohibition has failed; drugs are everywhere. In most urban areas of Britain it is easier to find illegal drugs than it is to find Kendal Mint Cake.

The problem is that users like drugs, and that makes outlawing them very difficult indeed.

TEN REASONS TO LEGALISE DRUGS

1. People take drugs. Why turn them into criminals? Save money on prison and spend it on treatment.

2. Spot the flaw in the logic that says: we shall teach drug users a lesson by putting them in prison ... where there are no drugs at all.

3. Illegal drugs are often impure. Ecstasy has been found mixed with heroin, making it a gateway drug to addiction, and cocaine is cut with baby milk powder, making life very difficult for liberals boycotting Nestlé products. Ending prohibition should improve drug quality; from a consumer angle this is a huge step forward.

4. Legal heroin can be sold in supermarket pharmacies, so users can get cheap, high-quality drugs and collect Nectar points.

5. Prohibition fuels gangsters, so legalisation means gangsters will lose a major source of money and power. Of course they will seek new illegal markets, but they will struggle to achieve the money and status that coke, crack and smack brought them when reduced to smuggling exotic pets. There is no rebellious cachet in wandering around festival campsites hawking wares with the plaintive cry of, 'Macaws and parakeets, macaws and parakeets.'

6. For *Daily Express* readers: if Class A drugs are cheap then users will have to commit less crime to pay for them, and reduced crime levels will bring down the cost of your household insurance.

7. Drug profits are so enormous that the government can produce drugs cheaper than gangsters and still put a whacking tax on them, putting an additionally high 'wanker tax' on cocaine.

8. We would need to find a new moral panic to fill the vacuum left by drugs. I suggest beards.

9. The problem with the legalisation of drugs is the free market would then step in, so we could end up with

L'Oréal crystal meth at one end of the market and Asda own-brand cocaine at the other. Somewhere in between will be Fairtrade cocaine, with middle-class liberals snorting lines to support collective farmers in Peru. So instead we should nationalise the drug industry. It is sensible and profitable – and nothing is guaranteed to deglamorise drugs quite like a state-run industry.

10. We could buy opium off the farmers in Afghanistan, thus giving them decent money, lessening the grip of the Taliban and enabling troops to come home quicker.

8

THE *DAILY MAIL* SHOULD BE FORCED TO PRINT ON THE FRONT OF EVERY EDITION THE WORDS: 'THIS IS A FICTIONALISED ACCOUNT OF THE NEWS AND ANY RESEMBLANCE TO THE TRUTH IS ENTIRELY COINCIDENTAL'

THE *DAILY MAIL* is not so much a newspaper as spite spat on dead trees. The paper's founder, Lord Northcliffe, admitted as much when he famously said he gave his readers their 'daily hate' and the paper has steadfastly clung to that dictum. Essentially it is a *Pravda* for Middle England, existing to promote one singular idea: that the hard-working British middle class are being exploited by degenerate, lazy people who are probably poor and frequently foreign, although it has a sideline selling Princess Diana memorial china plates.

The world inhabited by the *Daily Mail* is brimful of pregnant teenagers, travellers, migrants and homosexuals, often all one entity, conspiring to defraud taxpayers of their money from an increasingly gullible left-wing state, obsessed with political correctness and stopping children singing 'Baa Baa Black Sheep'. The cast of villains each has their identifiable wrongs: single mothers sponge off the state, asylum seekers have come to Britain for our generous benefits and teachers in state schools want to give sex education lessons to foetuses so they can abort themselves.

In a world like this, thank God the *Daily Mail* stands up for the taxpaying earners of Middle England.

However, when it comes to actually paying tax in the UK, the *Daily Mail* itself is not as forthcoming as it could be. The Daily Mail Group Trust states that its 'ultimate holding company and immediate parent company is Rothermere Continuation Ltd, a company incorporated in Bermuda'.[6] We can assume the Bermuda in question is the same Bermuda as the offshore tax haven and not any high-tax-rate Bermuda that might exist.

In addition, *Private Eye* alleges that Lord Rothermere is a 'non domicile', a tax status where a person can live and work in Britain but avoids paying their full share of tax here. Rothermere has refused to comment on this.

None of this has much to do with the essence of the policy. I just thought you might like to read it.

9

TO RANDOMLY ARM
OAPS WITH GUNS

THERE IS ONLY one surefire way to improve the quality of life for Britain's elderly population and that is to arm them, properly, with everything from Tasers and 9mm handguns through to AK47s. Want to try and rob an old dear of her pension? Think again! You could be staring down the barrel of an Uzi while a blue-rinse trills, 'I don't fucking think so, sweetie.' Meals on Wheels, you better up your game: someone wants venison with a cranberry and port reduction – give it them or leaden death will come at you from under a tartan travel rug quicker than you can say 'Bugger me with a *Countdown* dictionary'.

These scenarios have much to recommend them but the real reason to arm pensioners is that a state pension for a single elderly person is £95.25 a week or £4,797 a year. For an elderly couple it is £152.30 a week or £7,919.60 a year.[7] Put it another way: Sir Fred Goodwin, ex-CEO of RBS, walked away with a pension of nearly £1,000[8] a day. He gets in five days what an OAP on a state pension gets in a year.

Pensioners and various agencies have lobbied and campaigned to improve this. They have tried begging. They can't borrow. So now it is time to steal. Arming the elderly is not so much about protecting them from muggers but giving them the means to become the muggers. This policy is nothing short of creating a pensioner bandit army.

Who will they rob? I would recommend the banks. 'You can't have pensioners stealing from banks,' you may cry. Why not? The banks started it. We have subsidised them by over £1.3 trillion, public money that could be paying for pensions. Indeed, I would advocate the hunting of bankers by pensioners. Hordes of pensioners should descend upon the City (after 9.30am so they can use their bus pass).They will roam the streets of London's financial enclave, dishing out death from trolley bags. They will tie one end of a rope to the back of their Shopmobility scooter and throw the noose end over a lamppost. Bankers will hand over their bonuses or dangle like marionettes.

The pop of champagne corks in the City bars will cease at the sound of the click-clack of knitting needles and the gentle hum of a Dame Vera Lynn song.

And pensioners will get an increased pension, by all means necessary.

10

THERE SHOULD BE
A MAXIMUM WAGE

*S*AY THE WORDS out loud, 'maximum wage', and that popping sound you hear will be *Daily Telegraph* readers' capillaries bursting like blood-filled bubble wrap. The poor souls thought the world had ended when the minimum wage was reintroduced, so a maximum wage should finish them off.

'You can't introduce a maximum wage,' they cry, 'or the wealthy will leave the country.' Really? Can we have that in a legally binding contract? It's just that a lot of people have made these promises in the past and then let us down, so I propose a further amendment to this policy: anyone who says they will leave and then doesn't can be sued for breach of contract.

Amidst these empty threats of departure it is worth noting that the UK loses £18.5 billion a year in tax revenue to offshore tax havens – in corporate tax 'efficiencies', rich individual tax avoidance and tax evasion – so when the bankers start saying they will leave the country, feel free to point out that their money has had a head start.[9]

'Oh,' the bankers will moan, 'you can't have a maximum wage. If I don't get my bonus I won't feel motivated enough to work.' Most people manage to get out of bed and do a day's work without the promise of a Learjet at the end of a year, so what makes them so fucking special? 'We should get our bonuses,' they reply, 'because we are worth it,' thus confusing want with worth and reality with L'Oréal adverts. Push them a bit further and they will say, 'I'm only getting the market rate for the job,' forgetting that they set the market rate.

The maximum wage rate would be set using a formula, with the most anyone could earn set at ten times the national average wage. The national average wage is about £25,000, meaning the maximum wage would be £250,000, a quarter of a million. The joy of this is that if someone at the top of the salary scale wants to pay themselves more money, they have to pay everyone else more to raise the national average wage.

11

WINDSOR TO
BE RENAMED
LOWER SLOUGH

THE ORIGINS OF this policy lie deep within the twisted hearts of the inhabitants of Windsor, some of whom took exception to the fact that the Royal Borough of Windsor and Maidenhead shares the initials for its postcode with Slough. Part of Windsor has the postcode SL6 and part of Maidenhead has the postcode SL4, the SL in both instances coming from Slough. Those who took exception decided to start a local campaign to give Windsor and Maidenhead their 'own' postcode, which would be WM.[10]

Such is the importance of a postcode that some believed the SL of Slough was lowering the tone of Windsor and possibly, horror of horrors, lowering property prices! A simple SL bringing down the price of a house – how fantastic is that! If it's that easy let's start putting SL on other postcodes: Ascot for starters, then Henley, Chester, St Ives and Chipping Norton. Let's get those house prices down.

In response to the madness of snobbery, one of the good citizens of Slough decided we should change Windsor's name entirely and replace it with Lower Slough. This policy was adopted by the diverse and overly excited audience in Slough, who cheered the result so loudly that their whoops of joy could probably be heard in Windsor, thus knocking a few more quid off the asking price.

But the success of this policy is entirely in your hands, dear reader, as a place name only really exists in the minds of those who use it. Therefore let us eradicate the name of Windsor. If you have to send a letter to that area, address it to Lower Slough. Tell American tourists visiting our shores that they really should visit Lower Slough Castle and that if the flag is flying at full mast it means Elizabeth Lower Slough is at home.

And as the famous public school Eton College occupies the area between the castle and Slough itself, technically it is in central Slough. It only seems right, therefore, to rename Eton Slough Central College. It would be worth it just to see the number of their pupils getting in to Oxford or Cambridge plummet.

As John Betjeman should have said:

Come friendly bombs fall on Windsor
It isn't fit for nought but whingers
To rid of them we do avow
So rename it thus: Lower Slough

12

MPS SHOULD HAVE NO JOB OTHER THAN THAT OF MP

WHENEVER A MEMBER of Parliament is challenged on the issue of MPs having jobs outside Parliament, they throw their hands up in horror. 'No,' they cry, 'if you banned politicians from outside work you would end up with professional politicians with no experience of life.' There are few other jobs in the public sector where people are encouraged to moonlight as part of their job description. You don't see many teachers abandoning a class to give a speech for Swiss banking conglomerates, declaring, 'If all I did was teach you'd end up with very bland teachers.' Or bin men leaving work halfway through a shift declaring, 'I've got to write my weekly column.'

It is worth reminding ourselves that MPs are there to represent thousands of constituents, hold the government to account and run the country, which doesn't sound part-time to me. Are they really suggesting that managing a banking crisis, a recession, mass unemployment, troops in Afghanistan and a massive national debt of around £200 billion doesn't require their full attention?

Let us consider a few examples:

Ann Widdecombe, MP for Maidstone and The Weald, has a publishing contract, writes columns for the *Daily Express*, does numerous speaking engagements and presents the odd documentary. All of which, with her Parliamentary salary, earned her well over £244,000 last year.[11] That is quite a lot of 'life experience' to bring into Westminster. So it is a real shame she only managed to turn up and vote on less than half the votes held.[12]

George Galloway, MP for Bethnal Green and Bow, presents and appears on radio and TV shows and writes newspaper columns. That earns him, including his Parliamentary salary, over £229,000 a year.[13] All of which was so exhausting he only managed to speak three times in

Parliament last year and turn up for 8 per cent of the votes.[14]

Alan Milburn, MP for Darlington, spoke at an Avail Consulting event in June 2009 and was paid £9,200.[15] That same month he spoke in a debate in Parliament, and as that is the only time he spoke in a Parliamentary debate in a year, his earnings for that speech were £64,766.[16]

13

IF MPS WANT A SECOND JOB IN ORDER TO GAIN A GREATER UNDERSTANDING OF LIFE OUTSIDE GOVERNMENT, THEN THEIR CONSTITUENTS SHOULD CHOOSE WHICH JOB THEY THINK WOULD BEST EXPAND THEIR MP'S HORIZONS

SO IF MPs are to keep their other jobs, claiming it gives them greater experience of life, then we should be able to choose which job they get. If a democratic vote is good enough to vote them into one job, then it should be good enough to help them choose another. As the original proposer of this policy wrote: 'They could end up as a non-executive director for an oil company, a classroom assistant or a prisoners' plaything.'

Here are a few suggestions to be going on with:

Ken Clarke: Hod carrier. This is a kill or cure option.

Nick Clegg: Children's entertainer and balloon modeller. Not dissimilar from his day job as leader of the Lib Dems.

Harriet Harman: Community Support Officer. She deserves it, they deserve her.

Peter Mandelson: Pizza delivery boy.

Jacqui Smith: Avon lady. She'd enjoy having a good nose around other people's homes.

George Osborne: Dental nurse. Don't know why, it just seems right. Perhaps because he'd suit those blue disposable gloves.

David Cameron: Holiday rep in Faliraki.

Gordon Brown: Traffic warden in Lambeth.

14

THE POLICE SHOULD WEAR BADGES WHICH DISPLAY THE WORDS, 'HOW AM I POLICING?' AND 'I'M HERE TO HELP'

I T STARTED WHEN signs appeared on the back of thundering great 20-wheeled lorries, asking 'How am I driving?', as if the hairy-arsed truckers gave a monkey's for what some twat in a Prius two cars back thought of their signalling skills. And from there it exploded: every company, profession, government department and public body wanted to get 'feedback'.

I want to see 'How's my clowning?' badges on children's entertainers, with an 0800 number attached. Traffic wardens should be forced to wear badges saying, 'Ask me where the free spaces are.' I keenly await the cold-calling questionnaire that begins, 'On a scale of one to ten, where one is really dreadful and ten is utter shit, what number would you give Noel Edmonds?' I want bankers walking around the City with 'Thanks for the wages' or just 'My flash suit, paid for by you'.

Getting the police to wear 'I'm here to help' badges would serve as a reminder for all concerned. They would only have to catch sight of themselves in a shop window for a handy aide-mémoire, and protestors would feel able to approach them to ask if they can facilitate their legal rights to protest.

'How am I policing?' badges will then enable the public to provide feedback. So the facilitated protestor could phone and say, 'I've just had a very positive encounter with a police officer and I wanted to register my appreciation.' Unsatisfied customers (for instance, off the top of my head, those outside the Bank of England at the G20 protest) would be able to phone and say, 'Illegally'.

Finally, if the police are forced to wear badges saying 'How am I policing?', it might encourage them to actually display their numbers too.

15

AS TASERS ARE SO SAFE, EVERY TIME THE POLICE USE THEM ON A MEMBER OF THE PUBLIC THEY SHOULD TASER ONE OF THEMSELVES

WHEN TASERS (the electro-shock dart gun used by British police) were first used here it seemed that every other chief constable was lining up to get darted for the regional news, proving that electrocuting citizens was safe and that convulsing police officers make good television. One minute they would be twitching in agony and the next they would be explaining to the cameras that there was no long-term harm, while a PC discreetly burnt the soiled pants. All that's changed now, as the police have guidelines recommending they no longer Taser each other – for health and safety reasons. It's political correctness gone mad.

There are several clues, strangely not picked up by detectives, that electro-shock weapons might not be as benign as first thought:

Clue one: the description of Tasers changed. They used to be called 'non-lethal'. They are now called 'less than lethal', hinting that the weapon is not as 'non- lethal' as first suspected.

Clue two: the UK government regards electro-shock equipment as torture equipment if it is sold abroad.

Clue three: most UK weapons for export are categorised as 'controlled'. Electro-shock weapons are categorised as 'restricted' alongside WMD and long-range missiles. Let's be clear: electro-shock weapons are in the same category as anthrax and the plague.

Clue four: Amnesty International reported that between 2001 and 2008 370 people died after being Tasered in the US and Canada. In at least 50 cases, examiners listed being Tasered as a causal or contributory factor in the death.

Clue five: the standard for the police to use Tasers is 'just below lethal force' according to Keir Starmer, Director of Public Prosecutions. So they should be used where shooting someone dead is the only other option. But increasingly Tasers are being used as a tool of first resort. In Leeds, a 25-year-old man on a bus was slumped over his rucksack in a diabetic coma – the police Tasered him as they thought he might be a bomber, even though the Taser could have set off a bomb.

This policy will cause officers to be more thoughtful when deploying these weapons. This should reduce the misuse of Tasers and potential harm. However, when the weapons are regrettably used we at least get to see the return of the jolting PC to our TV screens.

16

TO INTRODUCE THE 1967 ABORTION ACT INTO NORTHERN IRELAND

NORTHERN IRELAND IS no newcomer to fighting progressive legislation, homosexuality being a case in point – legalised in 1967 in the rest of the UK but illegal in Northern Ireland until 1982. The delay was due in part to Ian Paisley's fantastically named campaign, 'Save Ulster from Sodomy'. (Paisley had nothing to fear personally: the picture of him screaming the word 'sodomy' immunised him from any such eventuality.)

But I confess to being shocked when the Belfast audience voted for the policy to introduce the 1967 Abortion Act into Northern Ireland. Until then, I thought that Northern Ireland operated under the same rules as the rest of the UK. But no, the law that applies in Belfast is the 1861 Offences Against the Person Act,[17] a statute that was created before women could even vote, let alone voice concerns over their reproductive rights. This law is so antiquated that Section 26 of the Act makes it an offence for a master or mistress to inadequately feed and clothe a servant.

Although women can get an abortion in exceptional circumstances, about 40 women a week travel from Northern Ireland to England for the operation. They can't get the procedure on the NHS, so have to go private and pay between £600 and £2,000.

Dawn Purvis, leader of the Progressive Unionist Party, says that 'the Labour government had a chance when they were putting through the Human Fertilisation and Embryology Act [2008]. An amendment was put down to introduce the '67 Act but that didn't happen. Leaders from the Northern Ireland Assembly wrote to the PM and said if they forced abortion into Northern Ireland it would damage the peace process. How can affording women reproductive rights threaten peace?'[18]

Westminster unfortunately took the Assembly's threats seriously, rather than enjoying the irony that former supporters of terrorism have become ardent defenders of the 'right to life'. Neither did they see the irony of the Department for International Development's paper of October 2009, outlining their position on safe and unsafe abortion. It reads: 'In countries where it is legal, DfID will support programmes that make safe abortion more accessible. In countries where it is illegal and mortality and morbidity is high, DfID will make the consequences of unsafe abortion more widely understood, and will consider supporting processes of legal and policy reform.'[19]

So the British government is willing to support the fight for abortion rights around the world – just not in Northern Ireland, the one place where they could make most progress really, really easily.

17

EVERYONE SHOULD BE ENTITLED TO PHONE IN WORK ONE DAY A MONTH AND CLAIM A 'FUCK IT' DAY OFF

IN BRITAIN WE lose an incredible 27 working hours per person per year as a result of thinking of excuses for not going to work.[20] Inevitably, a distracted workforce lacking in focus and concentration has a direct effect on productivity and efficiency.[21]

Across Britain this amounts to significant reductions in profitability on a company level and a lowering of the Gross Domestic Product on a national level. This policy seeks to redress this by removing the obstacle to efficiency. Instead of wasting time thinking of ways to avoid work, we should simply provide employees with a viable and all-encompassing excuse: the 'fuck it' day.

Unlike the 'duvet day', the 'fuck it' day offers employees the option of leaving the house instead of remaining on the sofa, as there is no fear of being caught playing football or being found drunk in a pub at lunchtime.

What's not to like?

18

EVERYONE SHOULD BE GIVEN THE DAY OFF ON THEIR BIRTHDAY

EVERYONE DESERVES THIS policy. Consider the occasions when we do get days off. We have bank holidays – and frankly, if ever there was an industry that deserves to have its nose to the grindstone, it is banking. We celebrate Jesus's birthday and it's not as if he's around to have any cake. Then there is May Day, international workers' day, where we celebrate working people by not working. There are even days off to remember Jesus's death. We have holidays for all sorts of nonsense, while the one thing we don't get to celebrate is our individual selves.

Any sane and decent land would give folk the day off on their birthday. We therefore declare any employer who opposes this policy to be a flint-hearted curmudgeon of such Dickensian proportions as to make Sir Fred Goodwin appear a kindly Quaker by comparison. We further declare that such a person will more than likely have shunned the joy of love, family and friends in an obsessive vision of work-obsessed tyranny. They will die alone, their final gasps will be to an empty room, and their laying to rest will see no tears or sorrow. And just to really rub it in, we will declare the day they die to be a public holiday.

NB: For those who ask, 'What happens if your birthday is on a weekend? Can we get a weekday off in lieu?' I reply, look, let's just get the policy up and running, don't take the piss just yet.

19

THERE SHOULD BE SEPARATE LANES FOR PEDESTRIANS BASED ON THE SPEEDS THEY WALK AT, RANGING FROM A FAST LANE FOR PEOPLE WHO KNOW WHERE THEY ARE GOING TO A HARD SHOULDER FOR WINDOW SHOPPERS

CITY-CENTRE CONGESTION is not limited to petrol-fuelled traffic; most shows featured policy suggestions for dealing with the problems faced by pedestrians. These ranged from banning cars in city centres to the banning of OAPs at certain hours. Another policy was 'Pavements to be automated, with moving walkways', and, putting aside the faint whiff of a *Blue Peter* 'design a city of the future' competition, this proposal has one fundamental problem: the amount of people in a city centre would remain the same but now getting even less exercise. The automated pavement would essentially become a conveyor belt for human lard.

The policy that eventually won creates a three-lane pavement, based on the motorway model, the outside lane for the fast walkers and the inside for window shoppers and pushchairs. The middle lane will retain its traditional role of providing a home for the indecisive and those who really should be in the slow lane.

There will also be a pedestrian code taught to visitors, especially in large cities like London, with rules on standing on the right on tube escalators, waiting until people get off before getting on public transport, and teaching advanced emergency stop techniques when getting caught behind groups of Spanish students in Piccadilly Circus. It will also require teen visitors to fit indicator lights on the back of rucksacks, although this will have to be carefully coordinated with the police, who might overreact at the sight of a flashing rucksack in a city centre.

20

THE *DAILY MAIL* SHOULD BE FORCED TO PRINT THE WORDS 'THE PAPER THAT SUPPORTED HITLER' ON ITS MASTHEAD

T HE *DAILY MAIL* currently denounces the British National Party and I am sure that old Lord Rothermere, one of the paper's original founders, would disapprove of them too, though in his case it would be because they were a bit tame. Old Lord Rothermere had a penchant for leaders who romped around Europe in the 1930s waving their right arm in the air, and wrote in support of them before his death in 1940.

Rothermere was an anti-Semite who visited Hitler on several occasions and excused the Nazi violence as exaggerated.[22] The fact that Rothermere wrote an article headlined 'Hurrah for the Blackshirts',[23] in praise of the British fascist leader Oswald Mosley, seems small beer by comparison.

The *Daily Mail* should be forced to print this on its masthead, although not because of a desire to stigmatise the paper, because frankly it has done a bang-up job on that task itself – it is, as Stephen Fry said, 'a paper that no one of any decency would be seen dead with'. Nor is it to indicate the *Mail*'s right-wing tendencies. (If you don't think the *Mail* is right-wing then you're probably a reader and there is little anyone can do for you.) Nor is it to serve as a reminder that the paper has a history of supporting orchestrated indignation. The real reason the *Mail* should print the words 'The paper that supported Hitler' on the masthead is just to ensure there is at least one piece of factual accuracy on the front page.

21

TO INTRODUCE A PROHIBITION OF DECEPTION ACT

THE QUESTION OF how we keep MPs honest was grappled in earnest by audiences the length and breadth of the country.

At least one policy every show declared that politicians should be hooked up to a lie detector every time they spoke in the House of Commons or were interviewed on the news. Indeed, most proposers went on to add that MPs should also be wired up to an electro-shock device that would be activated by untruths, though no one dared estimate the electricity bill, or considered the knock-on effects to the local economy as the entire borough of Westminster flickered on and off every Prime Minister's Question Time.

Quite a few policies were aimed at getting MPs to give a straight answer during interviews, and again it was mostly suggested that they be electrocuted if they failed to respond with a simple 'yes' or 'no' where appropriate.

One more imaginative soul suggested that all political interviews should be conducted under the rules of BBC Radio 4's *Just a Minute*, where MPs must answer questions without 'repetition, hesitation or deviation'. They would be awarded points for answering well and ... yes, you guessed it, electrocuted if they didn't. Presumably by Nicholas Parsons. It is fair to say that quite a few people just want to wire their MP to the mains regardless of their ability or integrity.

Of all the suggestions, the least violent is the Prohibition of Deception Act, a simple two-page private members' bill that seeks to make lying a criminal offence for MPs. In 2007 Adam Price MP backed the bill and got the support of nine or so other MPs. Or at least they said they supported it. Unfortunately the bill is no longer with us.

It read: 'It shall be an offence for an elected representative acting in this capacity, or an agent acting on his behalf, to make or publish a statement which he knows to be misleading, false or deceptive in a material particular.'

As this applies to the MPs' official capacity, it does mean they can continue to lie in normal everyday life. So from the classic, 'Honestly, that dress is perfect,' and 'I am really looking forward to the school play,' to the more exotic, 'I have never had sex with your brother under the family Christmas tree,' they would be able to lie along with the rest of us. But on important stuff like presenting the case for going to war, MPs could be arrested and put on trial for lying. For lovers of the traditional approach, we could wire them up when they took the oath.

22

POLITICIANS SHOULD
HAVE TO WEAR
TABARDS DISPLAYING
THE NAMES AND
LOGOS OF THE
COMPANIES WITH
WHOM THEY HAVE
A FINANCIAL
RELATIONSHIP, LIKE
A RACING DRIVER

W E NEED TO know in whose interest our MPs are working, so we can see who has dibs on them. Therefore
they must wear tabards with the names and logos of those
they have financial links with whenever they speak, both
inside and outside the House.

This doesn't just apply to companies that employ them
but all financial links. MPs can be given gifts, get free
tickets for events or travel, even get assistance to run
their offices, any of which could represent a conflict of
interest. So each and every one of the 'contributors'
should go on the tabards.

'Ah,' some will say, 'but MPs already have to declare this
in the Register of Members' Interests.' True. But how many
folk can be bothered to look it up? Are people up and
down the UK shouting from their living rooms, 'Ee, love,
come quick, and bring the Register of Members' Interests
– t'news is on and Oliver Letwin is talking on t'banking
system.' Wouldn't it be easier to see Oliver Letwin (Con)

standing on TV with Rothschild plastered on his chest next to KPMG and PricewaterhouseCoopers?[24]

If MPs wore the tabards they would continually be declaring their interests. So when Lembit Opik (Lib Dem) next stands up to talk about comets and asteroids colliding with Earth, we can see the *Daily Sport* logo and the Caravan Club of Great Britain emblazoned on his tabard.[25]

This policy is just the beginning. I believe that if MPs take money from companies they should be forced to sing that company's jingle whenever they stand to speak in the Chamber. That way David Blunkett (Lab) would have to sing the *Sun* newspaper's adverts every time he joined the debate.[26]

'Ah,' some may say, 'we should not be giving companies that kind of free advertising,' but the key here is positive advertising. I would argue that companies have more to lose than gain by displaying their brand on MPs. Frankly, the sight of Ken Clarke covered in British American

Tobacco logos is unlikely to influence anyone's behaviour. I doubt that kids would gather in the playground saying, 'Blood, d'you see Ken Clarke on that *Newsnight*?' 'Yeah. I'm gonna start smokin' cos he was sick, man!'[27]

23

THERE SHOULD
BE A PUBLIC
REFERENDUM BEFORE
GOING TO WAR

THIS POLICY ONLY applies when Britain is going to attack another country, not if someone attacked us, or we would have armed invaders charging up the beaches while we scampered around shouting, 'Fuck fuck fuck, we're not quorate ...'

A well-planned assault could overrun us before we had even got the ballot boxes out. We don't need a vote to prepare us to defend ourselves – a couple of ciders and an alcopop should do it.

Nor does this policy allow us to nominate countries we would like to invade. France, for example, has nothing to fear from this policy. The referendum applies to circumstances where a build-up of hostilities has been taking place over a period of time or where the international community[28] decide we need to act aggressively together.[29]

War by its very nature results in people getting killed (indeed any war without death is essentially the Duke of

Edinburgh Award scheme with alcohol) but those who lead us to war are the last to face the consequences of it. A member of one audience suggested we should develop an MPs' battalion, so as soon as they vote for war they are the first wave to be sent in – though looking at the state of our politicians this is not so much a military attack as a sacrificial offering. Atheists can regard it as giving the enemy a head start.

The decision to go to war is too important to leave to politicians, so it should be put to a referendum and voted on by the people whose children, relatives and friends will be the ones fighting the war.

In 2000 the Electoral Commission was tasked with conducting referendums and although they have not been run off their feet in that time, they are more than ready to hold a national vote should the prospect of invading a country and waging an illegal war based on false evidence and at the whim of the most detested president in US history ever present itself again.

24

THE PRIME MINISTER SHALL BE LIMITED TO TWO TERMS OF OFFICE

FOUR WORDS SUM up the argument for limiting a Prime Minister to two terms of office: Gordon Brown John Major. Had Margaret Thatcher and Tony Blair been limited to two terms of office then neither would have resigned mid-way through their third term. Both Brown and Major (initially) had their Prime Ministerial career foisted upon us unelected. They were not the first: Jim Callaghan became PM when Harold Wilson resigned in 1976, giving us three unelected PMs in the course of 31 years. An average of one a decade is pretty undemocratic for the mother of all Parliaments.

Other reasons for limiting the PM to two terms of office:

1. It stops them becoming too powerful and stops us becoming too familiar with them. When they are familiar, we get lazy as an elec-

torate and start voting on personality rather than policy.

2. The job of Prime Minister is simply too difficult to do well for more than two terms. It requires total concentration for every single waking minute. For proof, look at the state of them when they leave. Thatcher quoted Francis of Assisi going into Number 10 and dribbled on the way out. Blair entered looking youthful and full of hope and left looking like he was part of a hostage release programme having spent five years chained to a radiator.

3. They all go a bit mad after two terms. What did Tony Blair do for relaxation when he retired? He tried to restart the Middle East peace process.

4. If rotation is good enough for vegetables, it is good enough for politicians.

25

THERE SHOULD BE
AN AGE OF CONSENT
FOR RELIGION

ALL RELIGIONS ARE essentially cults with varying degrees of historical peer approval – the Church of England has Henry VIII, Catholics have St Augustine and the Scientologists have Tom Cruise. You can dress religious brainwashing up as spirituality or culture but it is still brainwashing. OK, it can teach you how to look alert when terminally bored and how to be thinking one thing and chanting another, both invaluable skills for a career in market research. But ultimately brainwashing by a cult is unacceptable as it can lead to a Channel 4 documentary.

If adults want to believe that the world was made in a celestial microwave powered by a divine space acorn, they have the right to do so. If they want to worship the acorn, pray to it and wear a golden acorn around their necks, that too is fine. But telling a child that unless they follow the Acorn Rules they will spend eternity being buried and dug up by demon squirrels is not.

This policy aims to balance the rights of religious freedom and the rights of the child by setting an age limit on religion. We cannot prevent parents from teaching their children about religion at home, so we should treat religion in a similar fashion to the old laws relating to pubs: children are not allowed into church, but parents can – perhaps with a meal or on a social occasion – allow some religion in moderation.

This policy will prevent children entering mosques, temples, synagogues and churches until they are 14 and will be enforced with a height bar, just like those at funfairs and adventure parks, with a little sign outside the church saying 'You have to be at least this high to go on this attraction'.

26

THOSE IN FAVOUR
OF ID CARDS SHOULD
BE BANNED FROM
HAVING CURTAINS

THOSE WITH NOTHING to hide have nothing to fear.

27

**ANYONE FOUND GUILTY
OF A HOMOPHOBIC
HATE CRIME SHALL
SERVE THEIR ENTIRE
SENTENCE IN DRAG**

THIS POLICY IS guaranteed to make homophobic criminals go straight ... or not, as the case may be.

28

**WHENEVER THERE IS
A BARNEY IN THE
HOUSE OF COMMONS,
THEY SHOULD PLAY
THE BENNY HILL
THEME TUNE**

THIS SHOULD ALSO be applied to council and regional assemblies. The Greater London Authority could play Chas and Dave's classic 'Rabbit', the Scottish Parliament gets 'Hoots mon there's a moose loose aboot this hoose', the Welsh Assembly Abba's 'Fernando' and the Northern Ireland Assembly could go for Black Lace's 'We're having a gang bang, we're having a ball'.

PRIVATE HEALTH COMPANIES THAT USE NHS-TRAINED STAFF, DOCTORS, NURSES, CLINICIANS, ETC., SHOULD PAY A LEVY WORTH 25 PER CENT OF THE STAFF PAY TO THE NHS TO REIMBURSE THEM FOR THE TRAINING COSTS AND HELP WITH TRAINING IN THE FUTURE

PRIVATE MEDICINE IS fundamentally un-British, as the only reason to use it is to jump the NHS queue – and the one thing we pride ourselves on as a nation is our ability to queue. It is what distinguishes us from the French. Therefore there is no greater social gaucherie or display of ill breeding than 'going private', as it is based upon an ability to push to the front shouting, 'Let me through, I have money.'

To compound this faux pas further, private health companies use NHS-trained doctors and nurses. Until private hospitals train their own staff, in their own medical schools, and corporate students push corporate beds around the West End to raise money for corporate rag week, the use of NHS-trained staff will always amount to a subsidy from the taxpayer to the private companies. It costs the state approximately £42,000 to train a nurse and approximately £240,000 to train a doctor, costs that the private companies do not appear to shoulder. So we should charge a levy on the private health companies to cover the cost of state training.

Everyone is a winner with a levy like this. The NHS gets funding for future training but the private health companies benefit too. By their very nature these companies are entities in the free market, which is at odds with a reliance on state aid. Sponging off the state in this hypocritical fashion must weigh heavily on their souls[30] and discarding it would have enormous therapeutic benefits for them, for which we won't charge them extra.

NB: Modern politicians really should take a glance at 1945, when Britain had the highest rates of national debt and yet, instead of cutting public services, created the National Health Service. Bloody marvellous.

TO INTRODUCE
A TOBIN TAX
ON CURRENCY
TRANSACTIONS

EVERY AUDIENCE, WITHOUT exception, had policies on what to do with bankers. In Bath one of the policy suggestions was simply 'Hang a banker every day of the year'. What struck me was not the orgy of violence but the orderliness. Underneath it was written 'and allotments for everyone'. How very British: a quaint mixture of bloodlust and gardening.

The most compelling banking policy that got widespread support was the Tobin tax. True, it doesn't sound too exciting, unless your name is Tobin, when you might feel picked upon, but essentially it is a payback from the City, a small way for a humble group of people to say sorry.

The global market for currency transactions is worth about $3.2 billion a day.[31] That's right, a day. It is untaxed and all we seek to do is set a tax rate of 0.005 per cent.[32] That is all. A global tax even of this size would raise between $30 and $50 billion a year.

Britain could introduce a Tobin tax on sterling without waiting for the rest of the world. Wherever sterling is sold we would simply apply this small tax via a global banking computer system that already exists. As the tax is applied only to wholesale currency markets (the inter-bank market) it does not affect the retails market, so there is no extra charge for converting currencies for sending money abroad or holiday cash. So your holiday pounds will still be worth as little tomorrow as they are today. A British Tobin tax would raise approximately $5 billion a year, money we could use to improve health and education. And the following year, when everyone is better and can read, get really pissed.

The Tobin tax is supported by Lord Adair Turner of the Financial Services Authority, the billionaire George Soros and French president Nicolas Sarkozy – but don't let that put you off.

31

ALL MEMBERS OF THE BNP SHOULD BE FORCED TO TRACE THEIR FAMILY ANCESTRY AND MAKE IT PUBLIC

IF THERE IS one thing the BNP dislike more than foreigners it is finding out that they themselves are foreign. What is the point of being a racist if your fellow racists are from the wrong race? It makes a mockery of the whole thing.

Over the past 2,000 years Britain has become a delightfully mongrel nation comprising of a good mix of French, Italian, Danish, Irish, German, Jewish, Romany, Asian, West Indian ... all sorts really. Over time and generations, things can get mixed up. This policy means the BNP will have to find out the exact racial make-up of those members from 'indigenous British ethnic groups'. I am sure they would appreciate it too. Isn't it important to know if a BNP member is stealing British jobs, taking British houses and shagging British women?

32

ALL MPS' SECOND HOMES ARE TO BECOME STATE PROPERTY AT THE END OF THEIR 'CAREER' (SECOND HOME = THE ONE CLOSEST TO WESTMINSTER)

THE AUTHORITIES CAN take the proceeds of crime from a criminal, so we have an established principle to retrieve the ill-gotten gains from MPs. Expenses are the reimbursement of legitimate costs, not perks, and no MP should personally profit from them. Westminster is set to phase out the payments for MPs' second homes, but it leaves two questions remaining.

Firstly, where should they reside when in London? One popular solution, which was voted into the Manifesto in Norwich, was to put MPs in a 'halls of residence'-type building when Parliament is sitting. As a solution it might seem tempting: relatively cheap, utilitarian and has a dash of rubbing the buggers' noses in it. Then you realise that if you shove 650-odd MPs in a dormitory together they will breed. This is a horrible thought, though the objection is not moral, it is purely a matter of taste. If you want your imagination hijacked with images of two old Labour backbenchers lustfully thundering to climax in their vest and socks, or want to visualise Tories dressed in Bullingdon club attire smeared in lard and amyl nitrate.

Another suggestion is that MPs should live in council houses, but there is such an enormous shortage of council housing that it would be unfair to take so many flats out of circulation. If an estate for MPs was created you just know it would be a beautifully kept gated community with a high security presence and the only graffiti would be a commissioned Banksy. Essentially it would be a state-funded luxury health spa with a Vauxhall Vectra on bricks in the forecourt for appearances' sake.

That leaves only one option left for the MPs: the Travelodge.

The second question: what to do with those MPs whose second homes have already been paid for by the taxpayer? This problem is easier to answer. The policy allows the state to reclaim existing second homes when the MP stands down, loses or dies. As MPs tend to live in more salubrious areas, their vacated property would make ideal council homes and provide a small start to replenishing our council stock.

33

THE GARMENT TRADE SHOULD PRINT THE AGE OF THE PERSON WHO MADE EACH ITEM IN THE LABEL

THIS IS SIMPLE. You can't pay a quid for a three-piece suit and expect to find a Fairtrade logo on it. Stuff doesn't come cheap if the person making it has pension rights or gets time off to go to school.

Perhaps surprisingly, 'cheap' doesn't always mean lowest standards: the 2009 report by Labour Behind the Label gave Gap and Primark a better write-up than Debenhams and John Lewis. Basically, globalisation – or as I call it MRSA capitalism – has enabled companies to outsource production to places with the cheapest labour costs, often places with no union rights, forced overtime, low pay and child labour.[33]

This policy aims to create greater consumer awareness by having two numbers displayed on a label – size of the item, then age of the producer. Shop assistants would be asked, 'Have you got this in a 14 years or older?' That's a whole new minefield for hapless men. Anniversaries would see partners returning gifts, saying, 'You know I'm an age 16, you'll have to take it back.'

The label can also silence moaning children on shopping trips when used in conjunction with the words, 'Some children actually work for their pocket money.' And if the teenager in your life is sloping around complaining about being bored, you can show them the label in your trousers: 'See? This boy is your age. He's made 30 pairs of chinos before you get up in the morning and if he had money for deodorant I bet he'd remember to use it.'

Another policy voted was, 'All products should have a photo of the person who made them sewn into the label. That photo should be taken at their place of work.' So if their work conditions were good you could have a 78-year-old Bangladeshi woman grinning at the back of your pants, which is a nice thought.

34

WE SHOULD ADOPT AN OPT-OUT SYSTEM FOR ORGAN DONATIONS

ACCORDING TO THE Chief Medical Officer, 'Every day at least one patient dies while on the transplant waiting list. There are something like 7,000 people on the waiting list at any one time. There is a shortage of organs in this country and the situation is getting worse.'[34]

The current system works on a donor card. If you die with a card, doctors can approach your next of kin and ask for permission to remove your organs. The only time the doctors get to ask is by its very nature the worst moment. In moments of extreme grief, relatives sometimes refuse the doctors permission regardless of the donor card.

The opt-out system simply assumes everyone has given their consent, unless they expressly opt out of the system and sign up to a register.

We would then have a much more plentiful supply of organs for donating, hopefully save hundreds of lives and in times of shortage the government can always change the speed limit to 120mph for motorcyclists, sit back and wait for the harvest.

35

THOSE WHO PEDDLE HOMEOPATHIC REMEDIES SHOULD ONLY RECEIVE HOMEOPATHIC MEDICINES WHEN THEY HAVE MAJOR ILLNESSES

WHO WOULD YOU rather have treat an illness: a person who has undergone medical training at medical school using peer-reviewed science and tried and tested clinical methods or a nettle-waving Hawkwind fan with a handwritten certificate?

Homeopathy claims to work by insisting that 'like cures like', so if your cold has symptoms like mercury poisoning, then mercury is the homeopathic cure. The mercury would be diluted in water until there was no mercury left, but miraculously the water would have a 'memory' of the mercury. The memory water will then be made into a pill.

So water has a memory, according to homeopathy, and if kids diluted their school text books they could cheat in class. Or perhaps I have wilfully misinterpreted the 'memory' of water and it has a more spiritual dimension, making the sewage system a highway haunted by ghosts, where just the memory of long-dead turds remains.

Either way it is bunkum. Simon Singh, a journalist who has written extensively on New Age quackery, says, 'There have been more than 200 trials investigating homoeopathy and the overall result is that its remedies are utterly bogus.'

This policy, that those who peddle homeopathic remedies should only receive homeopathic medicines when they have a major illness, takes the homeopaths' dictum at face value. If 'like cures like' then those that live by the water memory die by the water memory.

This would help weed out those homeopaths with the odd trace of self-doubt, and when the remaining peddlers get a major illness, a quick and painful demise is pretty much guaranteed. On the upside, we can dilute their remains and sell the memory water as a cure for ignorance. It is what they would have wanted.

36

CEOS AND BOARD MEMBERS OF ANY COMPANY CONVICTED OF FRAUD SHOULD BE FORCED TO DRESS AS PIRATES IN WHATEVER JOB THEY GET IN THE FUTURE

BRITAIN IS A newcomer to fighting corruption and bribery – after all, it only became illegal in 2002. It would have been made illegal earlier but someone paid a bung to keep it off the statute books and they were perfectly within their legal rights to do so. (Oh, all right, I'm making that bit up, though the 2002 bit is true.)

The first major company to be convicted under the new law were Mabey and Johnson, the Reading-based bridge-building firm, after they admitted bribing officials in Jamaica and Ghana and breaking UN sanctions in Iraq.[35] David Mabey, the CEO of Mabey and Johnson at the time, resigned from the board in 2008, but under this policy he would have to dress as a pirate should he wish to re-enter the world of remunerated employment. And properly like a pirate with a big pirate hat, a sash cummerbund thingy and a cutlass. He would also be forced to talk like a pirate. So if his new job was as a receptionist he would have to growl down the headset, 'Will you wait a minute while a salty sea dog like meself be putting you on hold.'

These pirate urchins would be able to wear normal clothes when not working, unless there was a business cross-over. For example, the Mabey group of companies made regular donations to the local Tory Party in Woking-ham; were David Mabey to attend Tory Party functions, the financial cross-over between his former business and the Tories would require him to wear his pirate daywear. Indeed, at Party Conference time, it's easy to suppose that business receptions would look like a Johnny Depp looka-like contest.

This policy forces us to take white-collar crime seri-ously, rather than excusing it as the price of doing busi-ness. My personal favourite is the prospect of the BAE Systems AGM commencing as the board take their places on the podium to the sound of wooden legs echoing around the room, followed by the mass squawking of a flock of parrots.

37

ANYONE WHO BUYS A SECOND HOME IN SOMERSET MUST BUY A HOME OF EQUAL WORTH AND GIVE IT TO SOMEONE WHO ACTUALLY LIVES IN SOMERSET

AMENDMENT 1. THIS HOME WILL BE BUILT UPON A GOLF COURSE

THE BRITISH COUNTRYSIDE is a thing of genuine and rare beauty, unfortunately ruined by the people who live there – or at least the people who drive there on a Friday night. The countryside of a weekend is essentially the City of London in green wellingtons, full of vile twats in cords who have come down to get the Range Rover muddy, walk the labradors and talk about boarding schools for their children. The type of people you hope are shot first in a hostage situation.

This policy was elected in Taunton but a very similar one was chosen in Exeter, probably because the south-west of England has suffered disproportionately at the hands of the City bonus and rich London knobs forcing up house prices beyond the reach of those who actually live there.

The south-west is the only part of England where house prices are higher than the national average but income levels are lower than the national average. In 2008, the average house price there was about 12 times the regional average wage. Between 2003 and 2008, the number of households on the waiting list for social housing has gone up by 43 per cent – one in every 14 households.[36]

So what can we do? One policy suggestion read, 'Reintroduce fox hunting, replacing foxes with bankers'; another, 'The entire population of Devon should invade the Docklands and squat in their homes just to see how they like it.'

The chosen policy, to buy a home of equal worth for someone who lives in Somerset, goes some small way to easing the housing crisis, rather than creating villages deserted during the week and full of braying hordes on a Saturday who think that being part of the community is joining the Countryside Alliance.

The amendment simply acknowledges that golf is shit.

TO INTRODUCE 'NONE OF THE ABOVE' ON BALLOT PAPERS

THE 2005 ELECTION saw Labour win 21.6 per cent of the eligible vote, while non-voters represented 38.6 per cent.

In 2001 Labour did slightly better, winning 24.2 per cent of the eligible vote, but non-voters won a stunning 40.6 per cent.[37]

Under current rules, the Labour Party were able to steal the last two elections, which were both won by anarchists, or a combination of anarchists and the apathetic. Fortunately for Labour, the Anarchists/ Apathy Alliance couldn't be arsed to claim victory, despite the fact that millions of voters didn't turn out to support them.

During the Manifesto tour, audiences often cheered the suggestion of having None Of The Above (NOTA) on the ballot paper: finally they saw the prospect of voting for something they wholeheartedly supported. There were amendments to NOTA, some preferring the words ReOpen Nominations (RON) instead, arguing that NOTA says 'Bollocks to the lot of you' and RON says 'Bollocks to the lot of you, we want this run again with proper candidates'.

However, both ideas are based on a simple premise. When you vote you give your consent to be governed, but consent can only be meaningful if you have a right to withhold it. If you applied the process of voting to sex, when Gordon Brown and David Cameron appear before us and say, 'Which one of us would you like to have sex with?', surely we have the right to say neither.

When I spoke to politicians about the prospect of NOTA, they were vehemently against it. 'Smaller parties will lose votes,' they said, or, 'It encourages voters to be lazy and not find out more about politics,' both of which might be true. But those arguments work the other way around too: if political parties get elected no matter what the level of voter turnout, then it makes politicians lazy. I think they will find all the motivation they need to reconnect with the electorate in the prospect of losing to an empty chair.

39

RENATIONALISE THE RAILWAYS

BRITISH RAIL WAS privatised in 1994 by John Major's Tory government, breaking up one single entity into over 100 different companies.

I once saw a grown man scream uncontrollably at a loudspeaker on a packed platform at Clapham Junction station. 'Liar!' His face was puce with rage and his overcoat flapped as he yelled, 'When. Will. You. Stop. Lying. To. Us!' It was a Friday afternoon, not yet five, and no one on the platform turned away or giggled in embarrassment. Instead they applauded. He got a round of applause for screaming at a box of wires and amplifiers. That is how shite our railways are.

A ticket for a train is a passport to a world of disappointment, humiliation, and yes, lies. The tickets are too expensive, the trains are overcrowded if and when they arrive, and we subsidise the private companies by nearly four times the amount we did when the thing was nationalised.

Average rail fares went up by 6 per cent last year (well above inflation), when we also saw the introduction of the most expensive ticket ever, the £1,000 fare from Cornwall to Scotland.[38] What will a £1,000 ticket guarantee? It will guarantee that you don't join the rest of us standing in a corridor which is thick with the smell of piss and shit. I can honestly say I have been in refugee camps in Africa with better sanitation.

Splintering the network has made our railways the most expensive in Europe. The reason for overcrowding is economic. Privatisation separated the rolling stock (carriages) from the train operators, so the train operator now has to lease the carriages; they make more money by renting fewer carriages and cramming us into smaller spaces. Conditions are so cramped that veal calves are protesting on our behalf.

And we heavily subsidise the only privatised national railway in Europe. For example, Virgin Trains received

£294.6m to run the West Coast mainline.[39] Giving Richard Branson a single pound coin in the street under any circumstances is wrong; giving him £294.6m to run a railway line is utter insanity.

GIVE US BACK OUR RAILWAYS, YOU LIARS.

(Or do I have to keep shouting at loudspeakers?)

GOATS ARE TO BE RELEASED ON TO THE FLOOR OF THE HOUSE OF COMMONS (NO MORE THAN FOUR); MPS ARE FORBIDDEN FROM REFERRING TO THEM EVER

I HAVE NO idea why this got voted through, nor what its purpose is, but as an act of surrealist sabotage it has a certain odd appeal.

NOTES

1. Blue is the correct answer.

2. 'Making London Safer', page 30, Boris Johnson, 2008.

3. http://www.taxresearch.org.uk/Blog/2009/02/01/tax-havens-cost-the-uk-185-billion-a-year/

4. Department of Work and Pensions. http://campaigns.dwp.gov.uk/campaigns/benefit-thieves/

5. Patricia Hewitt – Register of Members' Interests, Nov 2009 http://www.publications.parliament.uk/pa/cm/cmregmem/091111/091111.pdf

6. DMGT Half Yearly Report, page 35, point 23. http://www.dmgt.co.uk/mediacentre/newsreleases/20090521/5833/

7. http://www.direct.gov.uk/en/Pensionsandretirement planning/StatePension/Basicstatepension/DG_10014671

8. http://www.guardian.co.uk/business/2009/jun/18/rbs-sir-fred-goodwin-pension

9. See Policy 2 for remedy on this problem.

10. http://www.independent.co.uk/news/uk/this-britain/ windsor-wants-its-own-postcode-ndash-not-sloughs-773870.html

11. Register of Members' Interests. http://www.publications. parliament.uk/pa/cm/cmregmem/091111/091111.pdf

12. Theyworkforyou http://www.theyworkforyou.com/mp/ann_ widdecombe/maidstone_and_the_weald

13. Register of Members' Interests. http://www.publications. parliament.uk/pa/cm/cmregmem/091111/091111.pdf

14. Theyworkforyou http://www.theyworkforyou.com/mp/george_ galloway/bethnal_green_and_bow

15. Register of Members' Interests. http://www.publications. parliament.uk/pa/cm/cmregmem/091111/091111.pdf

16. Theyworkforyou http://www.theyworkforyou.com/mp/alan_ milburn/darlington

17. Offences Against the Person Act Section 59. http://
    www.opsi.gov.uk/RevisedStatutes/Acts/ukpga/1861/cukpga
    _18610100_en_3#pb7-l1g52

18. Interview with MT.

19. http://www.dfid.gov.uk/Documents/publications/Safe-and-
    Unsafe-Abortion.pdf

20. The figure of 27 hours was calculated using data-free analy-
    sis and para-factual science imaging.

21. The research that led to this conclusion was based on singu-
    lar objective result-led projections.

22. *Daily Mail*, 10 July 1933: 'I urge all British young men and
    women to study closely the progress of the Nazi regime in
    Germany. They must not be misled by the misrepresentations
    of its opponents. The most spiteful detractors of the Nazis are
    to be found in precisely the same sections of the British public
    and press as are most vehement in their praises of the Soviet
    regime in Russia. They have started a clamorous campaign of
    denunciation against what they call "Nazi atrocities" which,
    as anyone who visits Germany quickly discovers for himself,
    consist merely of a few isolated acts of violence such as are
    inevitable among a nation half as big again as ours, but which
    have been generalized, multiplied and exaggerated to give
    the impression that Nazi rule is a bloodthirsty tyranny. The
    German nation, moreover, was rapidly falling under the control

of its alien elements. In the last days of the pre-Hitler regime there were twenty times as many Jewish Government officials in Germany as had existed before the war. Israelites of international attachments were insinuating themselves into key positions in the German administrative machine. Three German Ministers only had direct relations with the Press, but in each case the official responsible for conveying news and interpreting policy to the public was a Jew.'

23. *Daily Mirror*, 22 January 1934: 'Timid alarmists all this week have been whimpering that the rapid growth in numbers of the British Blackshirts is preparing the way for a system of rulership by means of steel whips and concentration camps. Very few of these panic-mongers have any personal knowledge of the countries that are already under Blackshirt government. The notion that a permanent reign of terror exists there has been evolved entirely from their own morbid imaginations, fed by sensational propaganda from opponents of the party now in power. As a purely British organization, the Blackshirts will respect those principles of tolerance which are traditional in British politics. They have no prejudice either of class or race. Their recruits are drawn from all social grades and every political party. Young men may join the British Union of Fascists by writing to the Headquarters, King's Road, Chelsea, London, S.W.'

24. Register of Members' Interests.

25. Ditto.

26. Ditto.

27. Ditto.

28. America.

29. With Britain and Spain.

30. I use the term lightly.

31. Bank for International Settlements (BIS) Triennial Survey for 2007. www.bis.org/publ/rpfx07.htm

32. This rate was tested in a small UK bank in conjunction with the campaigning group Stamp Out Poverty.

33. Labour Behind the Label, Let's Clean Up Fashion 2009 – the state of pay behind the UK high street. http://www.labour behindthelabel.org/images/pdf/letscleanupfashion2009.pdf

34. *Guardian*, 17 July 2007. http://www.guardian.co.uk/society/ 2007/jul/18/health.medicineandhealth

35. The company was ordered to pay £6.6 million in 2009.

36. National Housing Federation Home Truths 2009 – South West http://www.housing.org.uk/Default.aspx?tabid=288&mid= 835&ctl=Details&ArticleID=2524

37. http://www.ukpolitical.info/Turnout45.htm

38. Neil Clark, *New Statesman*, 2009. http://www.newstatesman.com/business/2009/11/railways-public-privatisation

39. Neil Clark, *New Statesman*, November 2009. http://www.newstatesman.com/business/2009/11/railways-public-privatisation